BUSES

by Jeffrey Zuehlke

Pull Ahead Books

Lerner Publications Company • Minneapolis

Dedicated to Ellie, my favorite driver

Text copyright © 2005 by Lerner Publications Company

This book is available in two editions:
Library binding by Lerner Publications Company, a division of Lerner Publishing Group
Soft cover by First Avenue Editions, an imprint of Lerner Publishing Group
241 First Avenue North
Minneapolis, MN 55401 U.S.A.

Website address: www.lernerbooks.com

Words in **bold type** are explained in a glossary on page 30.

Library of Congress Cataloging-in-Publication Data

Zuehlke, Jeffrey, 1968–
    Buses / by Jeffrey Zuehlke.
      p. cm. – (Pull ahead books)
    Includes index.
    Summary: Introduces buses, how they work, and for what purposes they are used.
      ISBN: 0–8225–1538–5 (lib. bdg. : alk. paper)
      ISBN: 0–8225–2380–9 (pbk. : alk. paper)
      1. Buses–Juvenile literature. [1. Buses.] I. Title.
II. Series.
TL232.Z84 2005
388.3'4233–dc22   2003020270

Manufactured in the United States of America
1 2 3 4 5 6 – JR – 10 09 08 07 06 05

It's time to go to school! How will you
get there?

The school
bus will take
you there.
Here it
comes!

People wait for the bus at the bus stop.
Why? Because the bus stops at the
bus stop!

Bus riders are called **passengers.**
Buses can hold many passengers.

The driver is in charge of the bus.
The driver gets you to school safe
and sound.

The path in the middle of the bus is
called the **aisle.** Where do you want
to sit?

See the door at the back of the school bus? That's the **emergency door.** Leave through the emergency door if the school bus gets in an accident.

Everybody sit down! The bus is ready
to go. The driver uses pedals to make
the bus move and stop.

The driver turns the bus with the
steering wheel.

Stay in your seat when the bus is moving. Don't bother the driver. The driver needs to watch the road.

A big engine makes the bus move.

Buses ride on wheels. Each side of a bus has one front wheel.

Buses are big and heavy. Each side of a bus has two back wheels.

The school bus's **signal lights** flash when kids are getting on or off the bus.

The stop sign on the side of the school
bus tells other drivers to stop. It helps
kids to safely cross the street.

The bus goes to the school. The
passengers get off the bus. The driver
will come back later to take them home.

Where does the bus go after it takes you to school? It goes to the **garage.**

The driver fills the bus with gas at the garage.

Buses can get dirty on the road. This bus is being washed. Soon it will be ready to take you home.

This bus isn't a school bus. This bus is called a **transit bus.** Anyone can ride on a transit bus.

Transit buses carry people around town. The sign on the transit bus says where it is going.

Do you have your money ready?
Riders have to pay a **fare** to ride the
transit bus. Put your fare in this box.

The transit bus is crowded. There are not enough seats for everyone. Passengers hold on to the rail to keep steady.

Some buses are **intercity buses.** They go from city to city. Some intercity buses drive all the way across the country.

VRR-OOM! VRR-OOM! Don't miss
the bus!

Fun Facts about Buses

- Large school buses can hold up to 84 passengers.

- Large school buses weigh between 27,000 and 31,000 pounds (12,247 and 14,061 kilograms).

- There are more than 450,000 school buses in the United States

- The Greyhound Bus Company is the biggest intercity bus company in the United States. The Greyhound Bus Company carries more than 20 million passengers each year.

- The Greyhound Bus Company has more than 2,300 buses around the country.

- Some fancy intercity buses have bathrooms and television sets.

Parts of a Bus

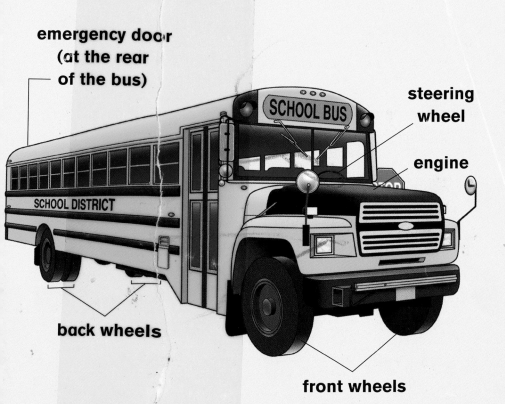

emergency door
(at the rear
of the bus)

steering
wheel

engine

SCHOOL BUS

SCHOOL DISTRICT

back wheels

front wheels

Glossary

aisle: the path in the middle of a bus

emergency door: the door at the back of a
school bus. It is used when there is an accident.

fare: money that people pay to ride a transit bus

garage: the place where buses are washed and
filled with gas

intercity buses: buses that carry people from
one city or town to another

passengers: people who ride on buses

signal lights: lights on a school bus that flash
when kids are getting on or off a bus

transit bus: buses that carry people around a
city, town, or small area

Index

About the Author

As a kid growing up in St. Paul, Minnesota, Jeffrey Zuehlke rode the bus to school. He always stayed in his seat and never bothered the driver. As an adult, he often rides the bus from his workplace in downtown Minneapolis to his home outside of the city. He still makes sure to stay out of trouble on the bus and *never* bothers his driver.

Photo Acknowledgments

The photographs in this book appear courtesy of: © Dennis McDonald/Photo Network, cover; © Kwame Zikomo/SuperStock, p. 3; © The Image Finders, pp. 4, 6, 7, 8, 9, 10, 11, 13, 14, 15, 16, 18, 20, 21, 22, 23, 24, 31; © Jim Baron/The Image Finders, pp. 5, 17; © O'Brien Productions/CORBIS, p. 12; © Howard Ande, pp. 19, 26, 27; © Stockbyte/SuperStock, p. 25.